The *Italian Sausage* Bible

*'My doctor told me to stop
having intimate dinners for four . . .
unless there are three other people!'*
ORSON WELLES

Share all recipes with three
others unless suggested otherwise.

The
Italian Sausage
Bible

Mary Contini

BIRLINN

First published in 2012 by
Birlinn Limited
West Newington House
10 Newington Road
Edinburgh
EH9 1QS

www.birlinn.co.uk

ISBN: 978 1 78027 050 0

British Library Cataloguing-in-Publication Data
A catalogue record for this book is available
from the British Library

Designed and typeset by Mark Blackadder

Printed and bound by Bell & Bain Ltd, Glasgow

Contents

Sausage recipes 33

The Silly Sausage, Sant' Antonio — the patron saint of the pig!

In spite of Garibaldi's unification of Italy over 150 years ago, the unique topography of the most blessed of lands has left its people and communities as independent and individual as ever. The Sicilian has nothing in common with the Tuscan, the Pugliese is a stranger to the Calabrese, even the citizens in Rome have little in common with those in the Vatican City!

From the remarkable and varied abundance of the land a food culture has evolved that is rich and diverse, built around local customs and traditions, intrinsically linked with Catholicism and primitive superstition.

There is no better way this can be demonstrated than the regional variations of the Italian sausage. There is barely a village or community which does not celebrate its own *salsiccie* — flavoured with a particular blend of spices, specific curing method or local ingredient that achieves its own unique character and flavour. Recipes are handed down over generations by word of mouth, jealously guarded.

The production of sausages as a method of curing pork is a tradition that can be traced back for centuries. Records show the ancient Romans prized 'Lucanica', a spicy pork sausage crafted in the southern region of Basilicata. These sausages were left as a single long casing, laid in a spiral rather than being separated into links. They were flavoured with pepper, cumin, savory, parsley, bayberry, whole peppercorns, 'plenty of fat' and pine nuts. The mixture was stuffed into washed pig's intestines and hung in caves to smoke. Today, an almost identical sausage, 'Luganega', is produced in northern Italy.

Pork remains Italy's favourite meat for curing. Pigs are especially prevalent in areas where there is a notable cheese-making tradition: after all, wherever there is cheese, there is excess whey, which, combined with bran and corn, becomes perfect feed for pigs.

In Tuscany we see the '*salsiccia finocchiona*', flavoured with seeds from the wild fennel that grows abundantly on the hillsides. They are usually eaten while fresh, prepared with beans or grilled and served with polenta.

Further south, the town of Norcia is renowned as the pork capital of Italy. Lying in the centre of Umbria's mountainous region, thickly populated with ancient oak trees, its hairy black pigs and wild boar were traditionally allowed to forage wild and feed on acorns, producing richly flavoured pork.

To the east, in Emilia-Romagna, the people are known as hearty eaters and are noted for their size and their appetites. They favour a rich, hearty cuisine which has been termed 'he-man's food'. The capital, Bologna, is famous for its mortadella – known as 'baloney' in the USA. Hailed as one of the greatest sausages in the world, mortadella is made

of finely chopped pork, kneaded well, cooked and highly spiced with black peppercorns and myrtle berries. Its origins stretch back to the Romans, who made a similar sausage called 'murtata', flavoured with myrtle or 'mortella' berries. References also occur in the fourteenth century, when the 'Guild of Sausage-Makers in Bologna' (how cool is that!) created a special mortar, *'mortaio delle carne di maiala'* for grinding the spices for this sausage, which may also have given rise to the name 'mortadella'.

Rumours abounded during World War II that mortadella was 'donkey meat'. Of course, it wasn't! Try eating it very finely sliced stuffed into a warm, fresh Italian panino and you'll never taste anything better.

Further south, in Lazio, where my family comes from, they make dried sausages flavoured with paprika, black pepper and fennel as well as other spices local to the hills around the villages. When our forebears emigrated to Scotland at the beginning of the twentieth century they brought the recipe with them. We use this same blend of spices today in Valvona & Crolla (www.valvonacrolla. co.uk) to make our own dried sausage, 'Fonteluna'®. This is a versatile sausage for all types of recipes, spicy and fairly hot, but good to eat raw or cooked, and it is obviously my favourite!

Things hot up even more when you get to Naples. Here they produce dried hot sausages packed with chilli and spice. In Lecce, the marble-walled city in the heart of Puglia, they make an unusual sausage that tastes of cinnamon and cloves.

In Calabria, barely a couple of hours' drive away, they make a spicy paste, 'miscela esplosiva', that is so hot it could blow your socks off! They use this to make the spiciest sausages of all.

To add to the mystery and tradition of the Italian sausage there is also fierce celestial competition among the holy saints, several of whom claim the prestige of being the patron saint of the Italian sausage!

The sour-faced Saint Ignatius has put his name forward, but he is too severe to carry it off. Good King Wenceslas would like to be known as the 'sausage king', though this is not mentioned in his popular theme tune. The honourable St Simeon, the patron saint of holy fools, wears a string of sausages around his neck like a wreath. Do you think he is trying to tell us something?

In Naples, on his feast day, to gain attention, San Gennaro makes a big fuss by miraculously liquefying his dried blood in a glass phial. Not a bad trick! He has a huge following, achieved in part with a bit of old-fashioned Neapolitan bribery. He insists his followers celebrate his great achievement by enjoying a huge, juicy, mouth-watering 'peperole and salsiccie panini'! He definitely draws the crowds with his ingenious marketing.

It is, however, Sant'Antonio who has claimed the top job and is the official patron saint of the sausage. As the holy protector of animals, Sant'Antonio is always depicted with his personal pet pig. A modest monk, he lived a simple, vegetarian lifestyle. But, like many holy vegetarians, he was constantly tempted by the devil to break his fasts and enjoy, of all things, hot, aromatic, sweet, juicy Italian sausage. Maybe the devil was in cahoots with San Gennaro!

Sant' Antonio's biggest temptation is on his very own feast day. On 17 January every year, every village in Italy slaughters its fattened pigs and makes a huge feast of . . . you've guessed it . . . sausages! These are no little piggies that went to market; they are magnificent beasts, 300 pounds or more, aggressive, snorting, thick-skinned. Once they meet their fate courtesy of the local butcher, they are scrubbed and butchered, and with the help of the whole family made into prosciuttos, pancetta, salami and sausages.

Poor old Saint Tony though . . . there'll be none for him! It's tough at the top.

Essentials

The secret of Italian cooking is the quality of the
ingredients used and the simplicity of the
flavourings added. A very limited selection of
essential seasonings can create the magic effect.

Aglio, olio e peperoncino

Garlic, oil and dried chilli . . . the ingenious combination.

Aglio, Garlic

There is an ancient myth that claims that when Satan left the Garden of Eden, garlic grew up in his left footprint . . . so the origin of the powers of garlic goes back a long way! In many cultures garlic has been regarded with both respect and suspicion. It has natural antiseptic and anti-fungal properties and apparently boosts testosterone. It is also regarded in many cultures, and especially in southern Italy, as a powerful force against demons, werewolves and vampires.

Treat garlic as a seasonal ingredient and use it sparingly. One clove, finely chopped, releases far more flavour than a dozen cooked whole cloves. When garlic cloves are cooked or baked whole, the flavour mellows into a sweet, almost nutty flavour that hardly releases any form of pungency. Raw garlic has the strongest flavour of all.

When sautéing garlic, be very careful not to burn it. The flavour turns intensely bitter.

Using finely chopped parsley with chopped garlic helps mellow the flavour.

Olio Extra Virgine, Extra Virgin Olive Oil

Extra virgin olive oil is an essential part of the healthy Mediterranean diet and is used in nearly all Italian cooking. It is a source of healthy mono-unsaturated fats and is high in Vitamin K, good for a healthy heart. Not only that, it tastes good and adds a delicious flavour to cooking.

It is best to choose cold-pressed extra virgin olive oil if you can. The different names for olive oil indicate the degree of processing the oil has undergone as well as the quality of the oil.

Extra virgin olive oil is the highest grade available, followed by virgin olive oil. The word 'virgin' indicates that the olives have been pressed to extract the oil; no heat or chemicals have been used during the extraction process, and the oil is pure and unrefined. Extra virgin olive oils are regarded as the healthiest and contain the highest levels of polyphenols and antioxidants.

Olives are harvested from November to January, and once pressed the oil lasts well up to 24 months but is at its best within the first year. Store olive oil in a cool, dark place.

Peperoncino, Dried red chillies

I use dried red chillis a lot in my cooking, a trick I learned from my Neapolitan grandmother. Used sparingly, they add a nice background kick to the flavour of recipes, not overpowering but instead balancing the sweetness of olive oil and garlic.

Buy fresh red chillis and string them up, hanging them in the kitchen to dry. They will last for months.

Parsley, sage, rosemary
and thyme . . . oh, and bay!

In all Italian regional cooking there is a natural affinity
between the seasonality of local food production and the
ancient traditions of fasting and feasting. Simply using the
right herbs adds an instant authenticity to the aroma and
flavours of a dish.

Nowadays we are used to using fresh basil, flat-leaf parsley and mint as flavour enhancers but with meats, game, pork and sausages it is the woody, aromatic herbs that create the best result.

They are at their best used straight from the plant, so it is worth investing in a woody herb garden. Choose the most popular plants to start with, and plant them either in your garden or, better still, in a few terracotta pots at the kitchen door or on a window ledge. The ones listed here are all evergreen and will flourish with your culinary pruning and supply you with fresh herbs for several years.

Bay Laurel . . .
Laurus Nobilis

A shrubby evergreen, grows to a small tree, used in winter to release a fragrant, perfumed flavour. Use it sparingly as it is powerful and aromatic. A word of caution: don't chew the leaves, they act as an intoxicant. You don't want to end up like the whacky ancient priestess who went wild after chewing bay leaves and 'rushed out in a full moon and assaulted unwary travellers and tore children and young animals to pieces'!

Rosemary . . . *Rosmarinus Officinalis*

An evergreen bush with beautiful purple flowers in spring, rosemary is perfect with pork and lamb, adding perfume and charm. Soft and fluffy in spring, drier and stronger favoured in the winter, always use fresh and liberally.

Sage . . . *Salvia Officinalis*

Ubiquitous stale dried sage is the ruin of many a stuffing. Use fresh leaves sparingly to add a bright, scented flavour to pork and stuffings. Use a few leaves to flavour melted butter as an ideal, easy dressing for stuffed pastas.

Infuse with a slice of lemon for a calming cleansing drink.

Thyme . . . *Thymus Vulgaris*

Plenty of small thyme varieties appear in gardens as evergreen foliage. Experiment with flavours and use sparingly but lovingly with roasts: pork, game, lamb, fish, sausages, potatoes and vegetables.

Fonteluna sausage®

My grandparents and great-grandparents were self-sufficient shepherds from the remote, mountainous regions of Lazio, between Rome and Naples. During the long, harsh winters they were often cut off from other villages for months, completely dependent on foods they had preserved and stored. The feast of Sant' Antonio in January, with its ritual slaughtering of the pig, was celebrated even more than Christmas, as this was halfway through the winter and produced an abundance of food that would last until spring.

When my grandparents emigrated to Scotland at the start of the last century, they came with nothing except the knowledge of their ancestors, their tenacity and capacity for hard work – and the secret recipe of their Italian sausages.

Named after their village, Fontitune, the sausages are now made to the same secret recipe and are enjoyed and celebrated here in Scotland. The recipe is still a secret . . . but we do sell it at Valvona &

Crolla if you would like to try it!

Italian sausages can be dried or fresh, spicy or mild. '*Salsiccia Paesana*' refers to any country-style fresh Italian sausages and can be spicy (piccante) or mild (dolce).

Italian sausages are usually made with 100% pork (70% meat, 30% fat) and are gluten-free, but can have lactose powder added; check the label when you buy them.

In the recipes that follow you can use any kind of Italian sausage, just use whichever type you prefer.

Make your own paesano Italian sausages

1 kilo fresh pork, belly, neck, shoulder (70% meat to 30% fat)
1 tbsp fennel seeds
1 tbsp black peppercorns
1½ tbsps sweet paprika
1 tbsp sugar
1 tbsp sea salt
1 tbsp red wine vinegar
Sausage skins, soaked in cold water, cut into 12–18-inch-long pieces
Butchers' string

When making fresh sausages you have to make sure your hands, equipment and surfaces are scrupulously clean. Make sure the pork is kept well chilled, as once it is minced there is a greater chance of bacteria spoiling the finished sausages.

Put all the pork and fat through a mincer to get a

coarse consistency (you can ask your butcher to do this for you).

In a pestle and mortar coarsely grind the fennel seeds and peppercorns.

Mix in the paprika, sugar and sea salt.

Lay the ground pork on a clean, flat surface and scatter the seasoning evenly across it.

Add to a bowl, add the wine vinegar and use your hands to mix everything together so the seasoning is well mixed through the pork. (You may want to use disposable latex gloves to prevent cross contamination.)

Fry a little of the mixture to check the seasoning, and adjust as necessary.

Pat the sausage skins dry with a kitchen paper and lay them out on a tray.

Use a funnel or sausage attachment on a food processor to push the pork into the sausage casings, massaging the sausages to make sure there are no pockets of air. If there are small pockets of air, use a sterilised needle to prick the casing to release the air.

Twist off the ends of the sausages and tie with string.

Refrigerate and use within 48 hours.

Fry or grill the sausages slowly and thoroughly to make sure they are completely cooked.

If you want to store the sausages for longer it's best to freeze them in small batches, as there are no preservatives in the mixture and they may spoil.

Cichetti culture

'Mangiando, mangiando; vieni l'apetito!', 'Eat and you'll get hungry!' In the north-east of Italy, early evening bar culture sees groups of workers or students sipping a glass of Prosecco, always enjoyed with little tasty 'bites' or 'cichetti'.

As you can imagine, variations of Italian sausages often appear.

Arancini rice balls with mozzarella and Italian sausage

250g Arborio rice
2 tbsps extra virgin olive oil
35g unsalted butter
300ml hot chicken stock
100g Parmigiano Reggiano, freshly grated
1 tbsp finely chopped flat-leaf parsley
2 eggs, beaten
Sea salt and freshly ground black pepper

For the stuffing
125g mozzarella di bufala, cut into 2–3cm cubes
2–3 mild Italian sausages, paesano dolce, fried gently until cooked and finely chopped
4–5 tbsps plain flour, seasoned
2 eggs, seasoned and beaten
4–5 tbsps fresh breadcrumbs

For frying
Sunflower oil or rapeseed oil

To make the rice balls
Add the oil and butter to a saucepan and add the rice, turning it in the oil for a few minutes.

Add the 300ml hot stock and stir occasionally as the rice cooks, absorbs the liquid and plumps up. Allow rice to cook for 20 minutes or so.

While the rice is still al dente, remove it from the heat and stir in the Parmigiano Reggiano, chopped parsley and beaten eggs. Check the seasoning.

Spread the rice on to a baking sheet and allow to cool, placing it in the refrigerator as soon as it is cold.

To make the stuffing
Mix the mozzarella and sausages in a bowl.

Lay the seasoned flour, beaten egg and breadcrumbs onto three flat plates.

Remove the cooled rice from the refrigerator.

Dust your hands with flour and pick up a walnut-sized portion of cold rice.

Make an indentation with your thumb and push in 2 tsps of the mozzarella and chopped sausage mixture.

Roll the rice into a small ball, and dip it first into the flour, then into the egg and finally roll it in the breadcrumbs so it is well coated.

Repeat with the remaining rice, placing the finished balls on a tray.

Place in the fridge again to firm up for at least 30 minutes, or up to 24 hours.

Heat some oil in a shallow frying pan, enough to fill it about a quarter full. When hot, fry the rice balls in batches, keeping a lively heat so that they brown nicely and are cooked right through.

Drain on greaseproof paper and sprinkle with salt.

The rice balls are best served warm.

Baked polenta with Italian sausages and mozzarella

Cook some polenta and leave to cool (see page 35).

Cut cold polenta into bite-sized cubes and drizzle with extra virgin olive oil.

Bake in a medium oven, 190°C/375°F/gas 5, with some spicy Italian sausages, paesano picante.

Cut the sausages into cubes and serve them warm, skewered together with the polenta cube and a small ball of mozzarella. Decorate with a leaf of fresh basil.

Bruschetta with broccoli and Italian sausages

Per person
75–100g purple sprouting broccoli or cime di rapa
Extra virgin olive oil
1 clove garlic, cut in half, half finely chopped
Small piece dried peperoncino, chilli
2–3 spicy Italian sausages, paesano piccante
Some finely chopped flat-leaf parsley
2 thick slices sourdough bread

Simmer broccoli in boiling salted water until just cooked.

Drain, refresh in cold water and roughly chop.

In a frying pan warm 2–3 tbsps extra virgin olive oil.

Add the chopped garlic and some spicy peperoncino, and warm through to release the flavours.

Chop the sausages into bite-sized pieces and cook gently in the oil for 10–15 minutes.

Add the chopped broccoli and cook together, adding a little more oil if necessary.

Add the finely chopped flat-leaf parsley.

Heat a griddle to high, lower the heat and griddle the bread till it is crispy with blackened ridges.

Rub the bread with the other half of the clove of garlic and drizzle with extra virgin olive oil.

Pile the bruschetta with the broccoli and sausage mixture, adding the juices from the frying pan.

Bruschetta with Luganega sausage and tomato

Pan-frying Italian sausages with a little extra virgin olive oil, a torn fresh bay leaf and a splash of water allows the sausages to stay soft and moist as they cook, while the bay leaf freshens the flavour and adds aroma.

Per person
100g mild Luganega sausage
1 fresh bay leaf
2 thick slices sourdough bread
Extra virgin olive oil
1 clove garlic
6–8 cherry tomatoes, chopped
1 dessertspoon black pitted olives, taggiasche or similar
Sea salt and black pepper
Fresh rocket leaves

Prick the sausages and pan-fry them with a little olive oil, a fresh bay leaf torn in half and a splash of water for 20 minutes until cooked.

Cut into slices lengthwise.

Dress the cherry tomatoes with a tablespoon or so of extra virgin olive oil and season with sea salt and freshly ground black pepper.

Add the pitted olives.

Mix in the warm sausages and their juices.

Heat a griddle to high, lower the heat and griddle the bread till it is crispy and has blackened ridges scored on it.

Rub the bread with the clove of garlic and drizzle with extra virgin olive oil.

Spoon on a generous spoonful of the tomato and sausage mixture and serve with plenty of rocket leaves that have been tossed in some olive oil and seasoned.

Bruschetta with mozzarella and spicy sausages

Per person
2 spicy Italian sausages, paesano piccante, sliced lengthwise
2 thick slices sourdough bread
Extra virgin olive oil
1 garlic clove
125g mozzarella di bufala, sliced
80g sliced stem tomatoes
Fresh basil
Sea salt and black pepper

Pan-fry the sausages with a tablespoon of extra virgin olive oil, a fresh bay leaf and a splash of water for about 20 minutes until cooked.

Add the sliced tomatoes to warm them and flavour them in the juices of the sausages.

Heat a griddle to high, lower the heat and griddle the bread till it is crispy and has blackened ridges scored on it.

Rub the bread with the clove of garlic and drizzle with extra virgin olive oil.

Season with sea salt and black pepper.

Top with slices of mozzarella and pile with the warm sausages and tomatoes and the juices from the frying pan.

Season, and dress with some sprigs of fresh basil.

Fonteluna sausage®
with green pickles

'Sottaceto' refers to anything that has been pickled in vinegar. Cured or dried Italian sausages can be eaten raw like salami and taste even better with spicy green pickles.

Makes about 10
200g Fonteluna or spicy dried Italian sausage
100g peperoni pickles, 'sottaceto'

Skin the Italian sausages and cut into bite-sized pieces.

Use a toothpick to skewer a peperoni pickle on top of the sausage.

Eat in one mouthful.

Italian pigs in blankets

How do you make a sausage roll? Push it down a hill!

300g mild Luganega or spicy Italian sausage (paesano piccante)

For the pastry
475g self-raising flour
1 tsp baking powder
Pinch of salt
340g unsalted butter, chilled and cubed
2 large free-range eggs, beaten
120ml buttermilk (or sour cream)
1 egg yolk to glaze

Pre-heat oven 200°C/400°F/gas 6.

Cut the sausages into equal lengths of 4–5cm and bake in the oven for 15–20 minutes until cooked, then remove and allow to cool.

Sieve the flour with the baking powder into a mixing bowl and add the salt.

Beat in the butter then the beaten eggs and the buttermilk to make a firm pastry.

Chill in the fridge.

Dust a clean work surface with some flour and roll out the pastry. Cut into 8–10cm squares.

Add a piece of sausage, cut to the length of the pastry.

Paint the edge of the pastry with beaten egg and cover the pastry over the sausage, trimming it so the sausages stick out a little at each end.

Seal the sausage rolls along their length by pressing the pastry together with the back of a fork.

Cut 2 diagonal slashes on the top of each roll and repeat till you have used up all the ingredients.

Lay the sausage rolls on a greased baking tray and brush with beaten egg.

Bake in the oven for 20–25 minutes until the pastry is browned and crispy.

You can use ready-to-cook puff pastry for a quick alternative.

Sausage skewers with rocket and lemon

Griddle some spicy Italian sausages, leave to cool.

Cut into slices.

While they are still warm, use a very thin lemon slice to wrap some rocket leaves round each piece of sausage.

Skewer two or three parcels on wooden toothpicks.

Potato croquettes with Italian sausage

---

3 spicy Italian sausages, paesano piccante
4–5 medium-sized floury potatoes, Maris Piper or King Edwards
Knob unsalted butter
2–3 tbsps grated Parmigiano Reggiano
150g melting cheese such as Fontina or Gruyère, cut into cubes
1 free-range egg, beaten
Sea salt and ground black pepper

Fry the sausages in a shallow frying pan until cooked.

Allow them to cool, then chop them very finely.

Boil the potatoes in salted water until soft. Drain well and mash with the butter.

Stir in the grated Parmigiano Reggiano, the cubes

of cheese and the finely chopped sausages.

Season well with sea salt and ground black pepper.

Add the beaten egg and combine to bind the mixture; cover and leave to cool in the refrigerator.

To make the croquettes
4–5 tbsps plain flour, seasoned
2 eggs, beaten and seasoned well
5–6 tbsps fresh breadcrumbs

For frying
Sunflower or rapeseed oil

Put the flour, beaten egg and breadcrumbs on separate plates.

Dust your hands with flour, roll the potato mixture into small sausage shapes, dust in flour, egg and bread-crumbs and set aside.

Heat the oil in a shallow frying pan and fry the croquettes on all sides until crispy.

Finish in a medium oven, 190°C/375°F/gas 5, so the mixture is warmed right through and the cheese is stringy and soft inside.

Roasted paesano sausages with mostarda di frutta

Mostarda di frutta are whole fruits such as mandarins, pears, cherries, figs preserved in a spicy sweet mustard syrup. They are a speciality of Modena and are used to accompany many of the pork products produced there. The town is the biggest producer of salami, prosciutto and sausages in Italy.

Bake mild Italian sausages, paesano dolce, in a medium oven (190°C/375°F/gas 5) and leave to cool.

Cut into bite-sized pieces and serve on skewers with whole pieces of spicy mostarda di frutta.

Sausage recipes

All-day paesano breakfast with polenta toast

Per person

2 mild Italian sausages, paesano dolce
4 slices smoked pancetta (or smoked streaky bacon)
2 juicy stem or plum tomatoes
2–3 tbsps extra virgin olive oil
1 clove garlic, peeled
4–5 chestnut mushrooms, cleaned and sliced
2 free-range eggs

Pre-heat oven to 180°C/375°F/gas 6.

Roast the sausages with the tomatoes until cooked.

Grill the bacon until it's crispy.

Warm the extra virgin olive oil and add the garlic to flavour.

Add the sliced mushrooms and sauté until they are soft.

Season with sea salt and black pepper.

Fry the eggs in a little olive oil . . . I like them sunny side up.

Serve all ingredients on a warm plate.

The polenta toast

Polenta is simply ground corn. It was unheard-of in Britain until around ten years ago, but is now a staple on lots of menus. Its great advantage is that it's cheap, quick (you can buy instant polenta) and gluten-free. I use soft polenta instead of mashed potatoes or pasta with lots of recipes. If you want to griddle it, it can be prepared in advance and left to solidify, just like cold porridge. Once solid, slice into fingers and brush with oil. Bake in the oven on a pre-heated griddle for about 20 minutes, turning it over halfway through. You can also sandwich it with cheese and bake it . . . a great snack.

To prepare the polenta
1 litre cold water
Sea salt
120g polenta

Bring the water to a simmer and add salt to taste.

Add the polenta in a steady stream, stirring in one direction with a long wooden spoon.

Once the polenta has absorbed the water, keep stirring for five minutes or so, then allow the polenta to cook a little. After that you can leave it to bubble gently for about 40 minutes, stirring only now and then to prevent a skin forming.

It is cooked when its texture is no longer grainy to taste.

Pour onto a flat plate and leave to cool.

Instant polenta is made the same way but takes only 5–10 minutes to cook.

Artichokes stuffed with breadcrumbs and Italian sausages

---

4 large artichokes
2 lemons

These artichokes are stuffed with seasoned breadcrumbs and steamed.

First prepare the artichokes: break off the coarse, spiky outer leaves until the white core is visible. Rub the pale surfaces with lemon juice so that they don't discolour.

Smash the artichoke head-down against a wooden board to open out the flower.

Use a small, sharp knife or the back of a spoon to scrape out the sharp, feathery choke in the middle. Rub inside with lemon juice.

Put the cleaned artichokes into a bowl of water with some cut slices of lemon while you prepare the stuffing.

To prepare the stuffing
Plenty of extra virgin olive oil
4 spicy Italian sausages, skinned and crumbled
2 cloves garlic, finely chopped
4 tbsps finely chopped flat-leaf parsley
8 tbsps dried breadcrumbs
Sea salt and freshly ground black pepper

Warm 2–3 tablespoons olive oil in a frying pan and sauté the crumbled sausage for 10 minutes or so.

Take it off the heat, mix in the garlic, parsley and breadcrumbs and season well. Add some olive oil to bind the stuffing.

Stuff the mixture into the cleaned artichokes, pushing the stuffing down between the leaves.

Sit the artichokes head up in a tight saucepan that will hold them all snugly.

Add a glass of cold water and a generous drizzle of extra virgin olive oil.

Bring to a simmer, cover the pan and leave to steam for 20–25 minutes until the core is tender and can be pierced easily with a knife.

Serve warm or at room temperature.

Barbeque Italian sausages with courgettes 'al cartoccio'

This recipe bakes fresh Italian sausages with courgettes in a foil parcel on the barbeque or in the oven; an easy, effective trick to capture all the flavours in one step. If you can, choose organic courgettes as they are usually crisper and less watery, so stay firmer when cooked.

---

6 fresh mild Italian sausages, cut into thirds
3–4 tbsps extra virgin olive oil
4–6 organic courgettes, washed and cut into the same size as the sausage pieces
Splash of dry white wine
Sea salt and black pepper
Lemon and crusty, sourdough bread to serve

Lay out four sheets of foil about the size of an A4 sheet of paper and rub with olive oil.

Divide the sausages, courgettes and lemon pieces between each parcel and season with sea salt and fresh ground black pepper.

Drizzle with a little olive oil and add a splash of dry white wine.

Fold the edges of the foil together to make a tight seal, allowing enough space inside the parcel to trap the steam that will build up.

Tuck the parcels in the middle of the ashes of the barbeque and cook for 30 minutes.

Alternatively, place on a baking tray in a hot oven, pre-heated to 220°C/400°F/gas 7, for about 30 minutes, depending on the size of the sausages.

Serve each person with a parcel, opened to release some steam and flavoured with a wedge of lemon and plenty of chunky sourdough bread.

Boiled eggs and Italian soldiers

Per person
2 extra-large free-range boiled eggs
2 mild Italian sausages (paesano dolce)
2 slices white bread toast, buttered
Heinz Ketchup or saucy salsa rossa (see page 102)

Grill the sausages until cooked and crispy.

Boil the eggs for four minutes.

Serve in two egg cups.

Dip the sausages into the sauce, then into the runny egg yolk!

Attention!

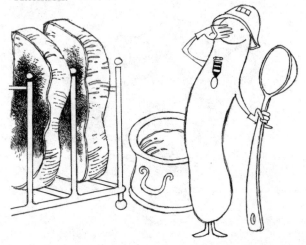

Bread baked with olives and Italian sausages

575ml hand-hot water
30g fresh yeast or 2 sachets instant easy-blend yeast
1 tsp sugar
1kg strong bread flour
25g Maldon sea salt
4 tbsps extra virgin olive oil
200g pitted black olives (taggiasche or similar)
200g Napoli sausage, skinned and finely sliced
Leaves stripped from 2 sprigs of fresh rosemary

Dissolve the yeast with the warm water and sugar and leave in a warm place for 10 minutes until it doubles in size. If using instant yeast check instructions on pack.

Use a food processor to make the dough. In a warm bowl mix the flour with the salt and oil and when the yeast has risen, mix it all with a dough hook for 10 minutes or so to make a warm, sticky dough that is smooth and elastic.

Rub the inside of a warm bowl with a little oil and turn the dough into it, covering the bowl with some clingfilm and cover with a damp cloth.

Leave in a warm place until it doubles in size, about one to two hours.

Punch down the dough and knead it again, dividing it into two round loaves.

Divide the olives, sausage and rosemary and work them into each loaf.

Place them on an oiled baking tray, cover again with a damp cloth and leave them in a warm place to prove again.

Pre-heat oven to 200°C/400°F/gas 6.

Bake in the top of the oven for 45–50 minutes until the bread is crispy and brown and has a hollow sound when tapped at the bottom.

BLACK OLIVES

Brussels sprouts with chestnuts and spicy paesano sausages

500g Brussels sprouts
Sea salt
4 tbsps extra virgin olive oil
2 cloves garlic, peeled
A small piece peperoncino
3 spicy Italian sausages, skinned and cut into small pieces
250g vaccum pack chestnuts, loosened
3–4 tbsps water
2 sprigs fresh rosemary

Prepare the Brussels sprouts and blanch them in boiling salted water for 5 minutes. Drain and refresh them in cold water.

Warm the extra virgin olive oil in a wide frying pan.

Sauté the garlic cloves and peperoncino, then add the sausage pieces.

Cook for 5–10 minutes until the sausages are starting to brown.

Add the chestnuts and Brussels sprouts and toss them in the flavoured oil so they are well coated.

Add the water and the rosemary and put a tight lid on the frying pan.

Cook everything for 20 minutes or so until all the flavours are combined and the sprouts take on a wonderful flavour . . . Italian magic!

Casteluccio lenticchie, braised spiced lentils

On New Year's Day it is lucky to serve lentils, as they are a symbol of money and wealth. (So is throwing old things out of your window and wearing red underwear!) Unless they are very old, the lentils should not need soaking before they are cooked.

250g brown lentils, Casteluccio or Puy lentils
3 tbsps tinned plum tomatoes
2–3 tbsps extra virgin olive oil
1 onion, very finely chopped
1 garlic clove
1 sprig fresh rosemary
1 fresh bay leaf
A few stalks flat-leaf parsley
Sea salt and freshly ground black pepper

To finish
3–4 tbsps extra virgin olive oil
1 garlic clove, finely chopped
1 piece peperoncino (dried chilli), crushed
2 tbsps flat-leaf parsley, finely chopped

Rinse the lentils, then put them in a saucepan with all the other ingredients.

Add enough cold water to cover. Bring to the boil and simmer for about 45 minutes, until the lentils are cooked and have absorbed all the water. (Add more water if necessary.)

Check the seasoning and discard the garlic clove and herbs.

To transform the flavour of the lentils heat some extra virgin olive oil in a frying pan and sauté the chopped garlic and peperoncino briskly, without burning. Take off the heat, add the chopped parsley, then stir the mixture into the lentils.

Cotechino with casteluccio lentils and mostarda di frutta

Cotechino is an iconic spiced pork sausage made of the rind, fat and scraps of pork seasoned with cloves, cinnamon and pepper. The original recipe dates back to around 1511, when the people of Gavello, a hill-top village in north-east Italy, were besieged and starving. When they had to slaughter their last pig they had no choice but to eat every part. They came up with an idea to stuff the pigs' trotters with every last morsel of left-over pork and season them with everything they had! The result is Italy's favourite sausage.

Today, all over Italy, cotechino is eaten on New Year's Day, served with spiced lentils and mostarda di frutta, a condiment made of whole fruits candied and preserved in a mustard-flavoured syrup. This is one of the tastiest meals of the year!

Serves 4
500g cotechino
Casteluccio lentils (see page 44)
Mostarda di frutta

Cotechino is a cooked product and only needs to be poached in its packet in simmering water for half an hour according to the manufacturer's instructions. (Dare I say it, not unlike a tasty version of haggis!)

Once it has been heated through, remove it from its silver pouch, drain the juices away and serve 2–3 slices per person.

Serve with some braised, spiced lentils and the sweet mostarda di frutta.

Cream of mushroom soup
with Luganega sausages

2 tbsps extra virgin olive oil
2 sticks celery, peeled and finely chopped
1 onion, finely chopped
1 clove garlic
400g chestnut mushrooms, peeled and sliced
2 medium-sized floury potatoes, peeled and diced
1.5 litres hot water
200g Luganega or mild Italian sausages (paesano dolce)
Sea salt and ground black pepper
Finely chopped flat-leaf parsley

Warm the oil in a saucepan and sauté the onions, celery and garlic.

Once softened, add the mushrooms and cook until softened.

Add the potatoes and warm water and cook until the potatoes collapse.

Remove the herbs and garlic clove, and liquidise the soup.

Remove the skin from the sausages and chop very finely.

Add to the soup and season, adding more water if necessary.

Cook for 20 minutes and finish with some finely

chopped flat-leaf parsley and an extra drizzle of extra virgin olive oil.

And . . . use a sprinkling of 'shak'o'chini' porcini mushroom powder to add an extra boost to the mushroom flavour.

Griddled Italian sausages on skewers

8 spicy Italian sausages (paesano piccante or Tuscan sausages), cut into thirds
2 red peppers, de-seeded and cut into quarters
2 red onions, peeled and cut into quarters
4 lemons cut into quarters
10 fresh bay leaves
Extra virgin olive oil
2–3 tbsps dry white wine
6 metal skewers or wooden skewers, soaked in water for 20 minutes

Pre-heat griddle or grill to high, then turn heat down to medium.

Skewer the sausages with the onion, red pepper, lemon and bay leaf, nestling each beside the other to hold in place.

Season with sea salt and freshly ground black pepper.

Brush with a little olive oil.

Place on griddle and cook through, turning so that all the ingredients cook evenly and are charred slightly on the outside. Splash with the white wine to keep the food moist.

Serve with a mixed Cos and Little Gem salad dressed with lemon juice and extra virgin olive oil.

Il panino di San Gennaro con salsiccie e peperoni –

San Gennaro's Italian sausage and peperoni roll

In the year AD 305, at the command of 'Dragonizio', the Persecutor, the unfortunate San Gennaro had his head chopped off just outside Naples. His legacy lives on in this recipe for the tastiest sausage roll on earth. Add some saucy salsa rossa (see page 102) and it could blow your head off!

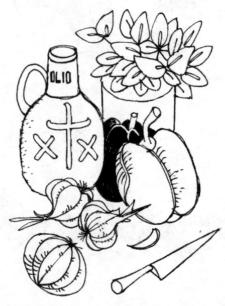

400g spicy Neapolitan Italian sausages
4 red peppers
2 red onions, finely sliced
4–5 tbsps extra virgin olive oil
1 clove fresh garlic, thinly sliced
Sea salt
Fresh basil
4 Italian panini

Pre-heat oven to 220°C/425°F/gas 7.

Skin and slice the sausages lengthwise and lay on a baking tray.

Remove stalk and seeds from peppers and slice thinly, lengthwise.

Lay on the baking tray, adding the sliced red onions, and scatter with the slices of garlic and a generous sprinkling of sea salt.

Add the extra virgin olive oil and mix together with your hands so everything is well coated with oil.

Roast in the oven for 20 minutes until the sausages are sizzling and the peppers and onions are softened.

Sprinkle with some torn basil leaves.

For the panini
Open the panini and fill each one to bursting with warm juicy, spicy sausages and a huge spoonful of the juicy, intense 'slurpy' peperoni and onions. Pour any juices over the filling.

Involtini di manzo with olive oil mash

Beef slices stuffed with pork sausage and peperoni, cooked in tomato sugo

For the involtini

2 whole red peppers
8 thin slices braising steak, cut for beef olives
1 clove garlic, finely chopped
2 tbsps finely chopped flat-leaf parsley
1 tsp fresh thyme leaves
250g Luganega pork sausages, cut into 8 pieces

Prepare the peppers by searing them on a gas flame until the skin is blackened and the flesh is softened. Peel off the blackened skin, or put the peppers in a plastic bag: the skin will stick to the bag and peel off easily. Slice the peperoni into slivers.

Lay out the slices of steak.

Season them well with plenty of sea salt and ground black pepper. Scatter with chopped garlic, chopped flat-leaf parsley and a few leaves of thyme.

Add some slivers of peperoni and share some of the sausages in each.

Roll them up and secure with a toothpick or skewer.

For the sugo
4–6 tbsps extra virgin olive oil
1 clove garlic
1 piece peperoncino
1 finely chopped Spanish onion
The involtini prepared as above
100ml dry white wine
2 × 450g tins Italian plum tomatoes, sieved
Fresh basil

Warm the extra virgin olive oil in a saucepan.

Add the garlic and peperoncino, and warm through.

Add the onion and cook gently until it is softened
and translucent.

Raise the heat and brown the involtini.

Add the white wine and allow the alcohol to
evaporate.

Add the sieved tomatoes and cook covered for
about an hour.

Add some water if the sauce gets too thick.

Season with sea salt and freshly ground black
pepper.

Add some fresh basil.

Serve these with olive oil mashed potato (see page
56) or with soft polenta (see page 34).

Italian bangers and mash

8 fresh Italian sausages, Tuscan or Paesano
Extra virgin olive oil
100ml dry white wine
2 cloves garlic, bashed
Fresh rosemary
Fresh bay leaf

Pre-heat oven 220°C/400°F/gas 7.

Lay the sausages on a roasting tray and drizzle with olive oil.

Add the dry white wine, the garlic cloves, some sprigs of rosemary and a few bay leaves and roast for 20–25 minutes.

For the olive oil mashed potatoes
600g floury potatoes (King Edwards or Maris Piper)
4 tbsps full fat milk or single cream
4–5 tbsps extra virgin olive oil
Sea salt and ground black pepper

Boil the potatoes in salted water until cooked, then drain.

Add the milk or cream and mash over a low heat.

Add the olive oil, using a fork to combine it with the mixture.

Season, and serve piping hot with the roasted Italian sausages and their juices.

Italian sausage and grilled tomato panini

Per person
2 floury Italian panini
2 mild Italian sausages, 'paesano dolce'
1 tbsp extra virgin olive oil
½ clove garlic, finely chopped
6–8 cherry tomatoes, halved
A few basil leaves
Sea salt and freshly ground black pepper
Heinz tomato ketchup or saucy salsa rossa (see page 102)

Grill the sausages until crispy.

Warm the olive oil in a small frying pan and sauté the garlic and tomatoes until softened.

Season with sea salt and black pepper.

Add a few fresh basil leaves.

Split the rolls and add a sausage and some tomatoes.

Drizzle with the juices and flavoured oil from the frying pan.

Serve with a dollop of sauce.

Italian sausage frittata

My Nonna, my mother's mother, made this frittata on
Good Friday with 33 eggs, an egg for every year of the
Lord's life. But without Italian sausage, obviously! No
meat on Fridays!

2–3 tbsps extra virgin olive oil
1–2 large shallots, finely chopped
250g spicy Italian sausages, Fonteluna, skinned and sliced
6 large free-range eggs
2 tbsps grated Parmigiano Reggiano
Sea salt and freshly ground black pepper
2 tbsps chopped parsley

Choose a heavy-bottomed 15–16cm/6 inch non-stick
frying pan.

Warm the olive oil and sauté the shallot until
softened.

Add the sausages and fry until lightly browned.

Beat the eggs; add the grated Parmigiano Reggiano
and season lightly with sea salt and black pepper.

Mix in the chopped parsley.

Pour the eggs into the frying pan and cook over a
low heat until the mixture sets.

Put a large plate over the frying pan and turn the
frittata onto it.

Turn the plate over and slip the frittata back into

the frying pan to finish cooking on the underside.

Serve warm. Great for a picnic: cool and wrap in kitchen foil, don't refrigerate.

Italian sausage tortilla

3 large potatoes, boiled in salted water, drained and cooled
3–4 tbsps extra virgin olive oil
1 large Spanish onion, thinly sliced
250g spicy Italian sausage, Fonteluna, skinned and sliced
6 large free-range eggs
2 tbsps finely chopped flat-leaf parsley
Sea salt and black pepper

Cut the cold potatoes into 2cm cubes.

Choose a heavy-bottomed 18–20cm/6 inch frying pan.

Warm the oil and cook the onions slowly until they are softened and slightly browned.

Add the sliced Italian sausages and potatoes, turn them in the oil and cook for a further 15 minutes.

Beat the eggs, season with sea salt and freshly ground black pepper.

Mix the chopped parsley into the eggs and pour into the frying pan.

Cook slowly for 20 minutes or so until the eggs are set.

Turn the tortilla over and finish cooking on the other side.

Great for a bullfight! Cool and wrap in kitchen foil. Don't refrigerate.

Italian sausages roasted with fennel

2 large heads fresh fennel
6 fennel-flavoured fresh Italian sausages, skinned and cut into thirds
Fennel herb
2 red onions, finely sliced
2 cloves garlic, squashed
4–5 tbsps extra virgin olive oil
Sea salt
Aniseed flavoured liqueur

Pre-heat oven to 220°C/400°F/gas 7.

Remove the outside tough parts of the fennel bulb.

Cut the bulb into quarters and cut away the coarse core.

Keep the fennel fronds to one side.

Lay all the ingredients in a heavy-bottomed baking tray.

Add the oil and use your hands to make sure everything is well coated with oil.

Sprinkle with sea salt and bake for 25 minutes until the fennel is cooked.

Bring the baking tray out of the oven and toss everything so it is all well roasted on all sides.

Add a splash of Anice Forte, aniseed liqueur or Sambucca, a splash of water and the fennel herb fronds you set aside earlier, and return to the oven for five minutes.

Italian sausages with white beans and tomato sugo

The Tuscans are known as 'mangiafagioli', the bean eaters. Charming!

2–3 tbsps extra virgin olive oil
2 garlic cloves, crushed
1 small piece peperoncino
6 fresh Tuscan Italian sausages
½ glass dry white wine
450g tinned plum tomatoes
450g tinned cannellini beans, drained
Fresh sage
Fresh rosemary
Sea salt and black pepper

Warm the olive oil in a wide, shallow saucepan, add the garlic and peperoncino, and cook for a few minutes.

Add the sausages and cook slowly to lightly brown them and release their juices.

Raise the heat and add the white wine and let it cook rapidly to evaporate the alcohol.

Add the tomatoes and use the back of a wooden spoon to break them up as they warm through and start to cook.

Sauté for 20 minutes or so before adding the drained beans, a few fresh sage leaves and a couple of sprigs of rosemary.

Season well with sea salt and plenty of ground black pepper.

Cook covered for 20 minutes, adding a splash of water if they look dry.

Serve with plenty of crusty bread.

Italian toad in the hole

For the batter
250ml semi skimmed milk
150g plain flour, sieved
2 large free-range eggs
Sea salt and freshly ground black pepper

For the sausages
2–3 tbsps extra virgin olive oil
1 clove garlic, chopped
2 large red onions
6 mild Italian sausages (paesano dolce), chopped
2 sprigs fresh rosemary

Pre-heat oven to 180°C/375°F/gas 6.

Whisk all the batter ingredients together. Set aside.

Choose a heavy-bottomed, deep baking tin, approx 24 × 20cm.

Add 2–3 tbsps extra virgin olive oil.

Add the garlic, sliced onions and chopped sausages.

Bake until the onions are caramelised and the sausages start to brown.

Take the baking tin from the oven, sprinkle some leaves of rosemary onto it and pour the batter over the sausages.

Increase the oven temperature to 200°C/400°F/gas 7.

Place on the middle shelf of the oven and leave for

20–25 minutes before checking the toad in the hole has risen and the pudding is high and crispy.

Serve immediately.

Lentil and Italian sausage soup

2–3 tbsps extra virgin olive oil
1 clove garlic, finely chopped
1 small piece peperoncino
1 large onion, finely chopped
3 sticks celery, peeled and finely chopped
200g spicy Italian sausages, skinned and chopped
2 floury potatoes, peeled and chopped
200g dried Italian brown lentils or a 400g tin Italian brown lentils,
drained
2 tbsps tinned plum tomatoes
1 litre hot water
1 fresh bay leaf and a sprig of fresh rosemary
Piece of Parmigiano Reggiano rind (optional)

Warm the olive oil in a saucepan and add the garlic and
peperoncino.

After a few minutes add the chopped onions and
celery and cook until softened.

Add the sausages, brown a little in the oil, then add
the potatoes, lentils, tomatoes and hot water.

Finally add the bay leaf, rosemary and a piece of
rind of Parmigiano Reggiano to add extra flavour.

Season with sea salt and cook for ¾ hour until the
lentils have softened, adding more water if necessary.

If you are using tinned lentils, add them once the
potatoes have softened.

Check seasoning.

To finish: serve with freshly grated Parmigiano Reggiano, extra virgin olive oil and a tablespoon of finely chopped flat-leaf parsley.

And . . . to make a bigger soup you can add a couple of handfuls of 'ditali', short pasta tubes, and a further 500ml of hot water for the last 15 minutes of cooking. Check seasoning again.

Monkfish with Italian sausages and peperoni

400g monkfish, trimmed and cut into 4cm pieces
4 spicy Italian fresh sausages, cut into thirds
2 red peppers, de-seeded and cut into quarters
2 tbsps extra virgin olive oil
Sea salt and black pepper
8 fresh bay leaves
Metal skewers

Warm a griddle on the highest heat for 10 minutes, then lower the heat.

Place all the ingredients in a bowl, season and use your hands to make sure everything is well coated with the oil, but not too much or the griddle will smoke the house out!

Thread the monkfish, sausage, pepper and bay leaves onto the skewers, using the bay leaf to separate each group of three ingredients.

Cook each side on the griddle for 4–5 minutes until everything is cooked and charred but still juicy.

Mussels stuffed with Italian sausages and herbs

This unusual recipe originates from the Italian cowboys of the Maremmana National Park in southern Tuscany, where the meat-eaters of the hills join forces with the fish-eaters of the coast.

---

4 tbsps extra virgin olive oil
1 onion, finely chopped
450g tinned plum tomatoes, chopped
Small bunch fresh basil
6 tbsps fresh breadcrumbs
4 Tuscan sausages, skinned and crumbled
3 tbsps finely chopped flat-leaf parsley
Fresh thyme leaves
2 cloves garlic, finely chopped
1 free-range egg, beaten
Sea salt and black pepper
2–2.5 kg large mussels

Use a large shallow saucepan with a tight lid.

Prepare a light tomato sugo.

Warm the oil in the saucepan and sauté the onion until translucent.

Add the chopped tomatoes and the fresh basil, season with sea salt and lightly simmer for 25 minutes.

Clean and de-beard the mussels, discarding any that do not close when tapped.

Put them in a wide pot and cook over a medium heat with a lid on for five minutes until they have all opened.

Shake the pot now and then to make sure all the mussels cook evenly.

Remove from the heat and discard any mussels that have not opened.

Prepare the stuffing by combining the breadcrumbs, sausage meat, parsley, thyme, beaten egg and seasoning together and add a little water if the stuffing is too dry.

Stuff the mussels with a teaspoon of stuffing and use a string to tie them together.

Pre-heat a medium oven, 180°C/350°F/gas 4.

Lay the stuffed mussels on the tomato sauce.

Bake in the pre-heated oven for 30 minutes, basting the mussels from time to time.

Remove the string before serving.

Serve with olive oil potatoes (see page 56) or soft polenta (see page 34).

Neapolitan pizza with fresh Italian sausage and friarielle

Friarielle is Neapolitan bitter broccoli. You can substitute sprouting broccoli or anything green and leafy that you like!

Pizza dough (see page 91)
Tomato topping (see page 91)
1 buffalo mozzarella, drained and torn into pieces
3–4 anchovies preserved in oil
200g spicy Italian sausage
200g friarielle, cime di rapa or broccoli, trimmed and cooked in salted boiling water
Clove garlic, sliced
Piece dried peperoncino
2 tbsps pitted black olives (taggiasche or similar)

Pre-heat oven to 230°C/450°F/gas 8.

Give the oven at least 20 minutes to heat up. Put a baking tray in the oven so that there is a hot surface to put the pizza tray on.

Warm some extra virgin olive oil in a frying pan with some garlic and dried chilli.

Add the cooked greens and sauté for 10 minutes to flavour them.

Knock down the dough and flatten it out with your hands, pulling it into two round pizzas.

Drizzle a little olive oil on to the tray and lay the

dough on top, using your fingers to press out the edges. Divide the tomato over the dough, spreading it with the back of a spoon, and leave about 2cm clear around the edge.

Drizzle with some extra virgin olive oil and dress with some pieces of mozzarella. Dot the pizza with some pieces of anchovy, slices of fresh sausage, some chopped broccoli and a scattering of black olives.

Bake at the top of the oven for 15–20 minutes until it is crisp on the bottom, speckled brown at the edges and beautifully cooked and moist on top.

One-pot risotto with Italian sausages and tomato

This is an easy supper risotto that can be made in 20 minutes, no faff!

2–3 tbsps extra virgin olive oil
1 clove garlic
1 onion, finely chopped
4 spicy Italian sausages, skinned and chopped
4 tbsps tinned Italian plum tomatoes, chopped
320g Arborio rice
1.25 litres hot chicken or vegetable stock
Some Parmigiano Reggiano, freshly grated
Parmigiano Reggiano skin (optional)
Fresh basil leaves

Warm the oil in a saucepan.

Add the garlic and onion, and sauté until softened.

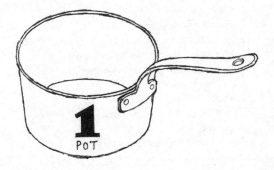

Add the crumbled sausages and sauté them for 10 minutes, before adding the chopped tomatoes.

Sauté for a few minutes, turning the tomatoes in the oil, and then add the rice.

Cook again for a few minutes, allowing the rice to absorb the flavours of the sauce.

Add the hot stock and the Parmigiano skin, stir, and allow to simmer for 20–25 minutes until the rice is cooked, adding a little water if the rice gets too dry.

Check seasoning, add some fresh basil leaves and serve with lots of freshly grated Parmigiano Reggiano.

Pasta and potato soup with Italian sausage

---

2 tbsps extra virgin olive oil
1 clove garlic, peeled
1 piece peperoncino
1 onion, finely chopped
2 spicy Italian sausages (paesano piccante), skinned and chopped
2 large floury potatoes, peeled and cubed
450g tinned plum tomatoes, liquidised
1 litre boiling water
Sea salt
3 handfuls short cut pasta (ditali)
Fresh basil
Freshly grated Parmigiano Reggiano

Warm the oil and add the garlic and peperoncino.

Add the onion and chopped Italian sausages and cook until onions are softened.

Add the potatoes, tomatoes and half of the boiling water. Season with sea salt.

Cook for at least an hour, until the potatoes have softened and collapsed.

Add the dried pasta and the rest of the water and cook until the pasta is al dente.

Add more water if the soup gets too thick, and check the seasoning.

Add some leaves of fresh basil and serve with freshly grated Parmigiano Reggiano

Secret trick: add a piece of the skin of Parmigiano while the soup is cooking to add a rich taste.

Even better secret tip: serve with a soft poached egg on each plate; the soup becomes a main meal!

Pastone Napoletana

On the 15th of August, every Italian family makes for
the hills and celebrates with a big 'scampagnata'!

As part of the picnic it is traditional to bring a
'pastone', a crumbly flaky pastry stuffed with ricotta and
spicy Italian sausage, a sort of majestic ham and egg pie.

Serves 8–10
2 × 250g packets frozen puff pastry
2 egg whites, lightly beaten

For the filling
4 large free-range eggs plus 2 egg yolks
250g ricotta or cottage cheese
100g Parmigiano Reggiano, freshly grated
Sea salt and black pepper
200g spicy Italian sausage, skinned and chopped
2 fresh bay leaves, broken into 4 pieces

To make the filling

Beat the eggs lightly with a fork, crumble the ricotta
into them and cream them together.

Fold in the grated Parmigiano Reggiano and season
the mixture well with salt and freshly ground black
pepper.

Preheat the oven to 220°C/425°F/gas 7.

Lightly grease an oblong tin, about 31 × 21cm and
3cm deep.

Pastone
Napoletana

VINO
DA
TAVOLA

Roll out one of the sheets of puff pastry and line the tin, rolling it thin enough to fall slightly over the edge of the tin.

Roll out the other sheet of pastry to make a topping for the pie.

Fill the pie with half the mixture, and sprinkle the chopped Italian sausage on top.

Lay the two egg yolks on to the mixture, one on each side of the pie.

Scatter the pieces of bay leaf over, then add the rest of the ricotta mixture, spreading it evenly.

Cover the pie with the second pastry sheet, brush the edges with the egg whites and pinch the pastry all around, sealing it well. Brush the top of the pastry with the rest of the egg white.

Score the top of the pie with a diagonal design, making a couple of holes in the pastry to let the steam escape.

Bake the pie in the preheated oven for 35–40 minutes until it is lightly browned.

When the pastry is browned and crispy on top, take the pie from the oven, use a knife to loosen round the edges, and invert the pie on to a wire rack. Tip the pie cooked side down back into the tin, so the base is now on top, and return it to the oven for another 20 minutes or so to let the bottom brown.

Cool the pie on a wire rack and eat it warm or cold.

Penne with paesano sausage sugo

3–4 tbsps extra virgin olive oil
1 clove garlic, peeled
1 piece peperoncino
1 large onion, finely chopped
4 mild Italian sausages, skinned and sliced
2 × 450g tins Italian plum tomatoes, liquidised
Sea salt
Fresh basil and Parmigiano Reggiano
320g penne rigate, or your pasta of choice

Warm the olive oil in a saucepan.

Add the garlic and chilli and cook gently.

Add the onions and cook until translucent, taking care not to let them burn.

Add the cut pieces of sausage and the tomatoes, and simmer for 45 minutes with the pot lid balanced on a wooden spoon to allow the sugo to evaporate a little.

Season with sea salt and add a few sprigs of fresh basil.

Cook the penne rigate (or your favourite pasta) in boiling salted water until al dente.

Drain and serve with the sugo and plenty of freshly grated Parmigiano Reggiano.

This sugo keeps well for 4–5 days in the fridge. Suitable for freezing.

Peperoni pizza ... twice

In New York, they call spicy Italian sausage 'pepperoni' or 'peperoni', but in Italy 'peperoni' are red peppers ... it leads to a whole lot of confusion when ordering a 'peperoni pizza'! Solution? Make a pizza with both!

Pizza dough (see page 91)
Tomato topping (see page 91)
Roasted peperoni (see page 54)
1 buffalo mozzarella, drained and torn into pieces
150g Napolitana Italian sausage, or spicy Fonteluna sausage®, skinned and sliced
Fresh basil

Pre-heat oven to 230°C/450°F/gas 8.

Give the oven at least 20 minutes to heat up. Put a baking tray in it so that there is a hot surface to put the pizza on.

Knock down the dough and flatten it out with your hands, pulling it into two pizza shapes.

Drizzle a little olive oil on to the tray and lay the dough on top, using your fingers to press out the edges.

Divide the tomato over the dough, spreading it with the back of a spoon, and leave about 2cm clear around the edge.

Drizzle with some extra virgin olive oil and dress with some pieces of mozzarella.

Dot the pizza with slices of fresh mozzarella, roasted

peperoni and several slices of Italian sausage.

Drizzle with some more olive oil.

Bake at the top of the oven for 15–20 minutes until it is crisp on the bottom, speckled brown at the edges and beautifully cooked and moist on top.

While still warm scatter with a few leaves of fresh basil.

Peperoni stuffed with Italian sausage

6 red peppers
6 tbsps extra virgin olive oil
6 fresh mild Italian sausages, paesano dolce, skinned and crumbled
100g fresh breadcrumbs
Nutmeg, sea salt and black pepper
2 tbsps chopped fresh marjoram
2 tbsps finely chopped flat-leaf parsley

For the topping
150g Fontina or Gruyère cheese, grated

Pre-heat oven to 220°C/400°F/gas 7.

Cut the peppers in half and de-seed them.

Rub them inside and out with extra virgin olive oil and lay on a baking tray.

Mix together the stuffing ingredients, seasoning the mixture well with a generous grating of fresh nutmeg, salt to taste and plenty of freshly ground black pepper.

Divide the mixture between the peppers and drizzle a little extra oil on top.

Bake in the oven for 30 minutes or so until the peppers are juicy and slightly blackened.

Remove and add a generous sprinkling of grated cheese on top of each pepper.

Return to the oven for a further 10 minutes until the cheese is melted and gooey.

Philip's Fonteluna sausage® sugo with rigatoni

After 30 years of marriage, my husband has started to cook for himself. Maybe he is trying to tell me something! He is extremely particular about 'his' sugo, which I have to say is very good!

---

8 tbsps extra virgin olive oil
1 large Spanish onion, very finely chopped
2 cloves garlic, finely chopped
150g Fonteluna sausage®

2 × 450g tins plum tomatoes
200ml cold water
2 fresh bay leaves
Sea salt

Warm the olive oil in a saucepan.

Add the onions and garlic and, with the lid on, sauté slowly for 15 minutes until the onions are completely softened.

Hold the Fonteluna under warm running water to loosen the skin, then score the sausage down each side. The skin will slide off easily. Slice the sausage thinly and add to the onions.

Cook for a further 10 minutes with the lid on, to release the sausage flavours into the oil.

Pour the tomatoes into a bowl and, after cutting away any coarse ends, chop them roughly and pour them into the saucepan with 200ml of cold water.

Bring to the boil and cook the sugo on a high heat for 10 minutes.

Lower the heat, add the bay leaf and cook gently for three quarters of an hour with the lid balanced on a wooden spoon to allow the sugo to reduce slowly.

Season with sea salt and ground black pepper.

Serve with 80g rigatoni per person, or your favourite pasta.

This sugo keeps well for 4–5 days in the fridge. Suitable for freezing.

Pina's gnocchi sardi pasta with artichokes and Italian sausages

Gnocchi sardi are a short, narrow-ribbed pasta shape typical of Sardinia, very good with chunky pasta sauces.

For the artichokes
4 fresh artichokes
1 clove garlic, finely chopped
2 tbsps finely chopped flat-leaf parsley
Sea salt
3–4 tbsps extra virgin olive oil
Lemon

The easiest way to prepare the artichokes is to start by breaking off the spiky outer leaves, working round until you see the yellow, paler leaves and heart.

Cut the artichoke into quarters and trim away the spiky choke in the middle.

Use a potato peeler to trim off any extra coarse leaves and dark green parts on the outside, which won't soften when cooked.

As you work, rub the outside of the artichokes with half of a lemon to stop them discolouring, and put the prepared pieces into a bowl of cold water.

Mix the garlic, parsley and salt together and rub onto the artichokes.

Lay them in a shallow saucepan and add 6–8 tablespoons cold water, just enough to cover the bottom of the saucepan by a couple of centimetres.

Drizzle the extra virgin olive oil over them and sauté them gently with the lid on until tender.

For the pasta sauce
Gnocchi sardi (80g per person)
3–4 tbsps extra virgin olive oil
2 cloves garlic, finely chopped
1 small piece peperoncino, crushed
4 spicy Italian sausages, skinned and crumbled
The cooked artichokes
2–3 tbsps finely chopped flat-leaf parsley
Pecorino Romano

Add the gnocchi sardi to the boiling salted water to cook.

Warm the olive oil in a shallow frying pan, and gently sauté the garlic and peperoncino.

Add the sausages and cook for 10 minutes or so.

Toss in the artichokes and finely chopped parsley.

As soon as the gnocchi sardi are al dente add them to the sauce, adding a spoonful of the cooking water to add moisture if the sauce looks dry.

Serve with grated Pecorini Romano.

Pecorino Romano is a salty hard sheep's cheese from Rome that adds a tasty, saltier flavour than Parmigiano Reggiano.

Pizza: all you need to know . . .
the dough and the topping

Makes 2 pizzas

For the pizza dough
350g organic strong white bread flour
210ml hand-hot water
1 sachet instant easy-blend yeast
1 tsp sea salt
Extra virgin olive oil

Warm a large mixing bowl.

Mix the yeast and salt into the flour and, using the handle of a wooden spoon, stir in the warm water, mixing to make a dough that leaves the sides of the mixing bowl clean.

Knead the dough either by hand or in a food processor for about 10 minutes until it is silky and smooth. Put it snugly into the bowl, drizzle a little olive oil over the top and cover the bowl with cling film. Put a damp tea towel on top and leave the bowl in a warm, draught-free place to let the dough rise and double in size for about an hour.

For the tomato topping
450g tin Italian plum tomatoes
2–3 tbsps extra virgin olive oil

Maldon sea salt
2 cloves garlic, peeled and sliced
2 tsps dried oregano

Chop the tomatoes roughly. Add two tablespoons of
extra virgin olive oil and season well with sea salt. Add
the sliced garlic and the dried oregano and leave to
marinade.

Pizza with mozzarella, tomato and Neapolitan Italian sausage

Pizza dough (see page 91)
Tomato topping (see page 91)
Extra virgin olive oil
1 buffalo mozzarella, drained
200g piece spicy Neapolitan Italian sausage, skinned and sliced
Fresh basil leaves

Pre-heat oven to its highest setting: 230°C/450°F/gas 8.

Give the oven at least 20 minutes to heat up. Put a
baking tray in the oven so that there is a hot surface to
put the pizza on.

Knock down the dough and flatten it out with your
hands, pulling it into two round pizza bases.

Drizzle a little olive oil on to the tray you are using

and lay the dough on top, using your fingers to press out the edges.

Divide the tomato over the dough, spreading it with the back of a spoon, and leave about 2cm clear around the edge.

Drizzle with some extra virgin olive oil and dress with pieces of mozzarella and slices of Neapolitan sausage. Add a few leaves of fresh basil.

Bake at the top of the oven for 15–20 minutes until it is crisp on the bottom, speckled brown at the edges and beautifully cooked and moist on top.

Rice, cabbage and Fonteluna® sausage soup

2–3 tbsps extra virgin olive oil
1 medium onion, finely chopped
Small piece peperoncino
200g spicy Italian sausage, Fonteluna or Napoli, skinned and sliced
Half a Savoy cabbage or similar, washed and cut into chunks
Boiling water
2 handfuls risotto rice or short pasta
Sea salt

Warm the olive oil in a saucepan.

Add the peperoncino, onions and sliced Italian

sausage and sauté for 5–10 minutes until the onions are softened.

Add the cabbage, stir it around in the flavoured oil and add enough boiling water to cover by about an inch. Simmer for half an hour.

Add the rice or pasta and stir, adding more hot water if the soup is too thick.

Check seasoning and simmer for a further 15 minutes until the rice or pasta is cooked.

Make a 'battuto'

This is a trick that transforms plain cabbage soup into something iconic!

2–3 thin slices of Italian lardo or unsmoked pancetta
1 clove garlic, finely chopped
1 small piece peperoncino, crushed
2 tbsps finely chopped flat-leaf parsley

Lay the lardo on a wooden board and bash it out with a rolling pin.

Scatter the garlic, chilli and parsley onto the lardo and bash them together.

Put this 'battuto' into the soup and simmer until it melts, thickening the soup and making the flavour rich and Italian.

Serve piping hot. This is even better left till the next day.

Roast chicken with Italian sausage stuffing and roast potatoes

1–1.5kg free-range chicken

For the stuffing
250g fresh ricotta
4 spicy Italian sausages, paesano piccante, skinned and crumbled
3 tbsp freshly grated Parmigiano Reggiano
2 tbsps finely chopped flat-leaf parsley
Squeeze of lemon juice
4 tbsps fresh breadcrumbs
Sea salt and freshly ground black pepper

For the chicken
2 tbsps extra virgin olive oil
3–4 sprigs fresh rosemary
2 lemons
1 kilo potatoes (King Edwards or Maris Pipers), peeled and quartered
2 shallots, unpeeled, cut in quarters
2 cloves garlic, unpeeled, but squashed
150ml white wine
Toothpicks or metal skewers

Pre-heat oven to 200°C/400°F/gas 6.

To time roasting the chicken, calculate 18 minutes per 500g plus 15 minutes or so extra to crisp up the skin.

Wash and wipe dry the chicken, removing the 'parson's nose' and any loose fat in the cavity.

Rub the bird all over with extra virgin olive oil and season well inside and out.

Mix all the stuffing ingredients together and season well.

Bind the mixture with a tablespoon of olive oil.

Stuff the cavity of the bird and close it by securing the bottom flap of skin over the opening with some toothpicks or metal skewers. (My Nonna used to sew the bird up, but she had nothing else to do all day!)

Place on a baking tray and add the rosemary and a couple of lemons, cut into quarters.

Roast in the medium shelf of the oven for about three quarters of an hour.

Remove from the oven and add the potatoes, shallots and garlic around the bird, spoon some of the juices over the breast of the chicken and make sure all the potatoes are coated in the juices.

Cook for a further three-quarters of an hour or so until the chicken is crispy and puffed up and the potatoes are cooked and irresistible.

Remove the chicken and potatoes to a serving dish to rest.

Add the white wine to the baking tray to loosen all the juices and make an easy gravy.

Serve the chicken with some of the stuffing drizzled with piping hot gravy.

Yummy! Yummy! Yummy!

Roast potatoes with Italian sausages, herbs and red onions

Probably the tastiest roast potatoes in the world!

---

1 kilo roasting potatoes (Maris Piper or King Edwards), peeled and cut into wedges
3 red onions, finely sliced
6 spicy Italian sausages, skinned and cut in half
3–4 cloves garlic, skin on and squashed
5–6 sprigs fresh rosemary
2 fresh bay leaves
4–5 tbsps extra virgin olive oil
3–4 tbsps dry white wine
Sea salt and black pepper

Pre-heat oven to 220°C/400°F/gas 7.

Lay all the ingredients on a heavy-bottomed roasting tin.

Pour the olive oil over and use your hands to mix everything together so it is all well coated with oil, then splash with the white wine.

Season well with sea salt and freshly ground black pepper.

Roast for 30–45 minutes until crispy and juicy, shaking the tin now and then so everything roasts evenly.

Salsa verde ... green sauce

1 large handful flat-leaf parsley
1 large handful fresh basil
1 tbsp salted capers (soaked in water for 20 minutes)
2–3 anchovy fillets preserved in oil
½ clove garlic, peeled
2 tbsps red wine vinegar
6 tbsps extra virgin olive oil
Sea salt to taste

Put all the ingredients into a food processor and give
them a short, sharp blitz to make a rough sauce.

Add extra oil if necessary.

Season to taste.

Good with roast meats, grilled
fish and grilled Italian sausages.

This sauce keeps well refrigerated
for 4–5 days.

Do not freeze.

Salsiccie cacciatiore, hunter's sausages!

'Cinghiale' or wild boar Italian sausages are full of flavour, and have a rich, gamey taste that goes well with tomatoes. You can imagine going out before dawn, hunting the wild boar, killing it, making the sausages, building a fire and cooking this dish!

Or for simplicity just buy the sausages. There is a lot of pent-up bashing going on in this recipe!

---

1 tbsp salted capers, soaked
3–4 tbsps extra virgin olive oil
3 cloves garlic, unpeeled and lightly crushed with the palm of the hand
2 onions, finely sliced
8–10 spicy Italian sausages, torn into thirds
3–4 tinned plum tomatoes, crushed
2 sprigs fresh rosemary
2–3 sprigs fresh sage
150ml dry white wine
2 tbsps stoned black olives, preserved in oil (taggiasche)

Soak the capers in a small cup of water to get rid of the salt.

Warm the oil in a wide frying pan and sauté the garlic.

Add the onions and cook slowly until translucent.

Throw in the sausages, toss them in the oil and after 5 minutes or so add the tomatoes and herbs.

Once the tomatoes have softened add the white wine, boil off the alcohol and add the olives and capers.

Cover and cook for 25–30 minutes, adding a little water if the sauce looks too dry.

Serve with crusty sourdough bread, olive oil mashed potatoes (see page 56) or soft polenta (see page 34).

Saucy salsa rossa . . . red sauce

3 tbsps fresh breadcrumbs
4 tbsps tinned plum tomatoes
2 fresh red chillis, de-seeded and chopped
1 tsp dried oregano
1 tsp red wine vinegar
2–3 tbsps extra virgin olive oil
Sea salt

Mix everything together in a food processor and add
enough olive oil to make a thick sauce.

Season with sea salt.

Good with roast meats, grilled fish and grilled
Italian sausages.

This sauce keeps well refrigerated for 4–5 days.

Do not freeze.

Sausages braised with
purple cauliflower

This Sicilian recipe from Mount Etna is called 'Sasizza
e u Bastardu'. Sicilian sausages are traditionally flavoured
with fennel seeds. The 'u bastardu' is a local purple
cauliflower which can be substituted with white
cauliflower.

6 spicy fresh Italian sausages, paesano piccante
150ml red wine
2–4 tbsps cold water
3–4 tbsps extra virgin olive oil
4 shallots, finely chopped
1 clove garlic finely chopped
1 piece peperoncino, crushed
6 anchovies preserved in olive oil, chopped
3 tbsps pitted black olives, preserved in oil (taggiasche)
1 cauliflower, separated into florets
1 tsp fennel seeds, crushed
A further 150ml red wine
Sea salt and black pepper
300g Provola cheese or mozzarella, shredded

In a frying pan brown the sausages and add some red wine and a few tablespoons of water.

Braise slowly to cook the sausages while keeping them moist and making a tasty gravy.

Warm the extra virgin olive oil in a separate frying pan and add the garlic and peperoncino, warm through then add the shallots and sauté until translucent.

Add the chopped anchovies, cook until they melt into the shallots, then layer the cauliflower florets in a single layer. Scatter the black olives and crushed fennel seeds and season with sea salt and freshly ground black pepper.

Cover with the red wine and a little water to keep the cauliflower moist and braise until the cauliflower is cooked.

Finish by adding the cheese, melt it through and serve with the braised sausages and their gravy and lots of crusty bread to mop up the juices.

Scallops with Fonteluna® sausages

12 large hand-dived Scottish scallops
Sea salt and freshly ground black pepper
200g Fonteluna sausage®, skinned and finely sliced
2–3 tbsps extra virgin olive oil
100ml dry white wine
Finely chopped flat-leaf parsley

Pre-heat a medium oven, 180°C/350°F/gas 4.

Loosen the scallops from the shells, rinse them and pat them dry.

Season them well with sea salt.

Wash the shells and pop them in a warm oven.

Warm the olive oil in a heavy-bottomed, wide frying pan and add the sliced sausage.

Cook to release their oils and flavours and turn them slightly crispy.

Remove and put in the oven to keep warm.

Raise the heat on the frying pan and sear the scallops for a minute on each side.

Add the white wine and quickly reduce it to evaporate the alcohol.

Serve the scallops in the warmed shells with some Fonteluna sausage®, some of the juices from the frying pan and a sprinkling of finely chopped flat-leaf parsley.

Spaghettini 'aglio e olio', with Italian sausages and broccoli

Probably the tastiest, fastest sugo on the planet!

---

1 head of broccoli
5–6 tbsps extra virgin olive oil
2 cloves garlic, finely chopped
1 small piece peperoncino, crushed
3 spicy Italian sausages, skinned and crumbled
2–3 tbsps finely chopped flat-leaf parsley
Spaghettini (about 80g per person)

Chop the broccoli into florets and blanch in boiling, salted water. Drain, refresh in cold water and set aside.

Warm the oil in a wide frying pan.

Add the garlic and peperoncino and sauté gently, taking care not to let the garlic burn. Add the crumbled sausages and cook for 15 minutes or so.

Add the broccoli and warm through in the spicy oil.

Cook the spaghettini.

While it is still al dente drain the pasta, leaving it quite moist, and add it quickly to the flavoured oil.

Toss everything together over a high heat, finishing cooking the spaghettini in the oil.

Add the finely chopped fresh parsley and serve.

And ... You can add freshly grated Pecorino Romano, which goes very well with these flavours.

Spaghettini with Italian sausage and bitter endive

Bitter curly endive, or 'scarola', is the winter version of summer frisée. The outer dark green leaves are strong flavoured and taste wonderful sautéed with garlic and chilli. The sweet flavour of pork is a perfect foil to the bitter taste of the greens. You could use curly kale or cavalo nero as an alternative.

---

1 head of scarola, winter frisée or endive
Sea salt
320g spaghettini
4 Tuscan sausages, skinned and cut into bite-size pieces
6–7 tbsps extra virgin olive oil
2 cloves garlic, peeled
2 pieces peperoncino
Freshly ground black pepper

Tear off the coarse green outer leaves of the scarola and wash in several changes of cold water. Cook in boiling salted water for 10 minutes. Drain and set aside.

In a large frying pan warm the oil and sauté the garlic and chilli.

Add the sausages and cook for 10 minutes or so.

Add the drained scarola and toss everything together.

Cook the spaghettini in boiling salted water until al dente.

Drain the pasta and add it to the frying pan, coating the pasta well with the sauce.

Add a spoonful of the cooking water if the pasta looks dry.

Serve with plenty of freshly ground black pepper.

Tagliatelle with Luganega sausage, mushrooms and cream

Fresh Luganega pork sausages from the north of Italy have a particular sweet flavour. They are mildly spiced with a hint of garlic, and marry well with mushrooms and cream.

2–3 tbsps extra virgin olive oil
1 garlic clove, finely chopped
1 shallot, finely chopped
250g Luganega pork sausage, finely chopped
300g chestnut or cremini mushrooms, wiped and sliced
3–4 ripe cherry tomatoes
250g egg tagliatelle
150ml double cream
Handful flat-leaf parsley, finely chopped
Sea salt and freshly ground black pepper
Freshly grated Parmigiano Reggiano

Heat the olive oil in a shallow saucepan.

Add the garlic and sauté for a few minutes to release the flavour.

Stir in the shallots and cook until they are soft and translucent.

Add the sausages and sauté until brown.

Stir in the mushrooms and tomatoes and cook slowly for 15 minutes or so, turning the ingredients in the oil.

Check the seasoning; as the sausages may be fairly salty, you might not need to add any extra salt.

Meanwhile, cook the tagliatelle in a large saucepan of boiling salted water until al dente.

Stir the cream into the sugo, then add the parsley and freshly ground black pepper.

Drain the tagliatelle, reserving some of the cooking water. Toss the pasta in the sugo, adding a little of the cooking water if it needs more liquid.

Serve with lots of freshly grated Parmigiano Reggiano.

Tuscan Italian sausages, mushrooms and tomato served with soft polenta

2–3 tbsps extra virgin olive oil
1 clove garlic, finely chopped
2 onions, finely chopped
1 piece peperoncino
300g chestnut mushrooms, cleaned and sliced
4 fresh Tuscan sausages, skinned and sliced
2 × 450g tins Italian plum tomatoes, roughly chopped
300ml cold water
1 sprig of fresh thyme
2 fresh bay leaves
Fresh basil

Warm the oil in a saucepan. Add the garlic, chilli and onions and cook until translucent and soft.

Add the sliced mushrooms and cook for 10 minutes, turning in the oil.

Add the sausages, and once browned a little, add the tomatoes and the water.

Pull the leaves from the thyme and add the bay leaves, torn in two to release their flavours.

Cook over a gentle heat for 30 minutes.

Check seasoning and add some sprigs of fresh basil.

Serve over a plate of hot polenta (see page 34) or olive oil mashed potatoes (see page 56).

Tuscan or Luganega fresh sausages pan-fried with red wine

2–3 tbsps extra virgin olive oil
1 clove garlic, peeled
1 Spanish onion, finely sliced
300g fresh sausages, Tuscan or Luganega
150ml dry red wine
100ml water
2 fresh bay leaves
2–3 sprigs fresh thyme leaves
Sea salt

Warm the olive oil in a frying pan.

Add the clove of garlic and after a few minutes add the sliced onions and sauté until the onions are softened and translucent.

Add the sausages and cook for 10 minutes until they start to take on some caramelised colour.

Raise the heat, add the red wine and cook at a high heat to evaporate the alcohol.

Turn the heat down, add the water and the fresh bay and thyme leaves and cook for a further 30 minutes or so until the sausages are cooked but still plump and juicy, and the gravy has reduced.

Check seasoning.

Serve with olive oil mash (see page 56) and salsa verde or salsa rossa (see pages 99 and 102).